D1282361

I Divorced My Money

&

Married My Mindset

This Time It's Personal

Dr. Tabatha Russell

Dedication

This book is dedicated to my loving family: My husband, children, and grandchildren. My parents, sister, brothers, and close friends.

My church family and spiritual mentors: Bishop Theotis & Elder Vernether White of Zion Hopewell Full Gospel Family Worship Center of Gilbert, SC; Bishop Graham & Minister Linda Graham of Life Connection of Concord, NC.

I am so grateful for each and every one of you that has given your support and encouragement over the years. You make me want to keep pushing and striving for a level of success that is unimaginable.

I pray that you will find your greatest level of success as you continue to pursue your purpose to the fullest. Be the best version of yourself... No Matter What!

Blessings!
Dr. Tabatha Russell

Foreword:

It has been a privilege to know Dr. Tabatha Russel for the past 20 years. We believe that God has raised her up at such a time as this to shift the mindset of this generation. In I Divorced My Money and Married My Mindset, Dr. Russell brings a timely and much needed message to the body of Christ. Each chapter unlocks the process by which we can fight the financial giant in our lives.

In I Samuel 17, the Bible speaks of David and Goliath. Everyone's mindset indicated fear, as seen in verse 24, "When the men of Israel all saw the man, they fled from him, and were very frightened." Goliaths mere size caused this mindset of fear. For many, money or the lack thereof creates that same Goliath-like fear. Like David, we must shift our mindsets and trust in God as he shares in verse 37, "The Lord who rescued me from the paw of the lion and from the paw of the bear, He will rescue me from the hand of this Philistine."

Through this book, we believe that every reader will be victorious in their pursuit towards shifting their mindset about money. Let go of fear and dive into your transformation today! This is a must-read.

Bishop & Elder Theotis White
Zion Hopewell FGFWC
Gilbert, SC 29054

CONTENTS

Introduction

Hello, Powerful Mind,

Welcome to another magnificent day in your journey called life. Have you ever wondered why you think the thoughts you think daily? I know that I have. Many of us think 6,200 or more thoughts per day. It is a known fact that 80% of the thoughts we think are negative. Not to mention that 95% of those thoughts are a repeat of the same thoughts from the day before. What we do with all of the thoughts we think determines our success or failure. As you read this book, imagine the possibilities.

This book was written with the desire that an extraordinary impartation will happen in your mindset to change generations. Our life's purpose is bigger than what we imagine at the moment. I found in my research that people with limited beliefs will never fulfill their dreams without changing from the inside out.

I dare you to make your shift happen! Don't let your narrative be average but be known for taking calculated leaps and bounds to greatness.

Love,

Dr. Tabatha Russell

Chapter One

The Discovery

Money is something that we all can identify with easily. It does not matter what country we live in, nor does it not matter what language we speak. Money is often perceived as having status or clout. Money is also that thing that is very attainable or simply unattainable. The thing that I see often is that people identify with money in two ways. (1) They identify with the ability to have millions and billions of dollars based upon their ideas, their inventions, their strategies, and the things that they have worked hard to accomplish. (2) The other thing is there are those individuals that identify with the lack of money and wander through life trying to find the golden ticket. They are looking for that one life-changing event that will propel their finances into millionaire status overnight. The chances that overnight financial success will happen without putting in the work is slim to none.

One day, I decided to divorce my money and married my mindset. What about you? Are you ready to decide that something needs to change? You see, depending on your childhood environment, very few of us can say that our parents were wealthy. In comparison, many more people will say they didn't have money growing up for their bare necessities. It is interesting how people compare what side of the tracks you were raised on. People don't even call it the right side of the tracks anymore. This is because of the distinct divide that has been placed between those that have a lot of money and those that don't. It seems like that conversation is meant for a selected few. What's the secret, you might ask? What are they talking about on the right side of the tracks that we need to know? Oftentimes, when we think about money, we think about how are we going to get it? Then, what type of job do we need to acquire in order to live a certain kind of lifestyle? As a child, it is often a dream and a fantasy to be rich. However, once you become an adult, the rubber meets the road.

As adults, we become so consumed with the need to have money that we miss out on great opportunities, or we do nothing at all to get the money that we once dreamed of having. The one thing that I found that makes the difference in whether or not we obtain money is our mindset. Our mindset tells us that we can or cannot do something. Our mindset will put us in a box, duct tape the lid, and put us on the shelf. When we break out from the cycle of being in a box, things begin to happen. Our limitations and boundaries become stepping stones as we propel to the next level.

I could imagine the top 2% richest people of the world who account for most of our nation's wealth have said a time or two that they want to be the world's richest person by any means necessary. With that being said, they may have looked at their situation and said I'm going to work as hard as I can, while I can. They go on to make things happen without excuses and without help if necessary. People with this attitude will fail many times on their way to becoming successful, but they don't quit. And as we've heard time and time again, even many inventors did not succeed on their first try, but they kept trying until they reached their perceived level of success.

Therefore, when we evaluate our mindset, we must take time to look at how we think and associate ourselves with things like money. One of the things that's helpful to do as you are evaluating your situation is to have a goal in mind. Start today... stretch towards that goal and every day align our thoughts with that end result in mind. Every day, do something towards that goal. And constantly remind yourself why. When I say why, I mean that you should have a reason why you want to obtain that goal. Why do you want to be a millionaire or a billionaire? It is a must that you have a solid reason for your why because it will help you on your journey when you have bumps in the road.

Your goals may require you to go a little deeper in your thoughts and actions. Once you get to the place of being a multi-millionaire, then what? What is the next goal? What is the next thing you want to accomplish? And how can you go back to help somebody else obtain that same goal and break outside of the box? Once you've learned how to shift your mindset, it becomes even easier for you to elevate your thoughts higher. This will allow you to grow in every area of your life. Just know that you're capable of doing whatever you set your minds to do. Right now, at this moment, you are all capable of making extraordinary improvements in your life and your environment. You can literally multiply your personal achievements to hit your personal best and go beyond the old limits that you set previously. There are no limits to what can be done.

The results that you can have may be tough for you to imagine right now, given your current situation. You are stronger than you think. Even if you don't feel strong right now, there is endless opportunity for you to become strong and resilient. You have the fighter within you that's needed to break out of the day-to-day cycles of negative thinking. Having limiting beliefs such as: you are not worthy or that you're not capable of achieving such high goals will paralyze your progress. Often, people will try to convince you that your goal is impossible when they look at your circumstances. For example, it's hard to think about becoming a millionaire or billionaire when you only have $1000.00 in the bank. It's really hard to think about what success looks like when you are broke or living one paycheck away from homelessness. No situation is so bad that you could not turn it around for the better.

The more that you are determined to work hard to obtain your goals, the easier it becomes. And the moment your mindset aligns with the goal that you have in mind, the journey begins. Things seemingly start to become a little bit easier along the way. You will find that you will start to come up with strategies that can help you become successful. You don't have to settle for things as you see them now. That can change literally overnight. If you're willing... life is prepared to give you a massive breakthrough experience. You can literally leap into higher realms of achievement. You will obtain those levels of success that you have always dreamt about... Once you're willing and if you're ready.

You don't have to be content with things as they are now or the achievements that you made in the past. That should only motivate you to want to go beyond to achieve greater achievements because of what you had previously done. Prior success should tell you that you're capable of going to the next level. Furthermore, the more that your mindset shifts, it will require far less effort than you've given in the past to face your fears or when you went bankrupt on the last idea. Fear might tell you to stop, but your new mindset will tell you to keep going because the next time just might be the one.

It may seem like a challenge to stay positive. But the fact that you were able to achieve success before is all the more reason why you should put forth the effort to do it now. Do you realize that you haven't begun to reach your full potential? And what is that anyway? How do you define success? How do you view your goals? How do you view your legacy? I believe that you may not have even begun to scratch the surface of what success looks like for you. Just know that one decision or one change in your mindset can allow you to proceed forward like never before.

Chapter 2

Time is equal

This is such a great time for you to pivot and shift your focus. What have you been waiting for? Have you been waiting on somebody to come and tell you that you can or can't follow your passion? Have you been waiting on someone to give you a hand up or permission to go to the next level? Have you been waiting on somebody to pat you on the back or somebody just to walk hand in hand with you to hold you accountable? Only you know the answers to those questions.

This is the time to fill in the blanks in areas of your life that have been holding you back. All of us have been given the ability to achieve greatness. Perhaps, you have been successful in some areas of your life previously. So, you know that success is possible. This is not the time that we stop and think about what went wrong in the past. This is the point that you know that all things are possible because of your hard work and commitment to your goals. All of us have 24 hours equally. We've been given the same amount of time to get things done. There is not a separate bucket of time for the rich and then a bucket of time for average people. Some people are extremely productive with their time, and others choose not to use their time wisely. The main difference between a rich person and a poor person is their use of time. You choose!

Write out what you will do to maximize your time to accomplish the goals you have set?

_____

_____

_____

_____

_____

_____

_____

_____

_____

_____

_____

_____

_____

_____

_____

_____

_____

_____

_____

_____

_____

_____

_____

_____

_____

_____

_____

_____

_____

_____

_____

The most successful people will tell you; it is not their money that they value the most. It is their time that they value. Successful people will say that time is one of their most valuable assets. Time is the one thing that you can't put a price tag on. Wherever you spend your time the most shows what you value. This stands true as to how you define and relate to success. There are a lot of millionaires that have gone flat broke and have been able to quickly bounce back from nothing. They realize that because they have been given time and another opportunity, they can bounce back. Time and energy combined can cause a combustible explosion in our realities. Such an incredible combination can shift how we look at things. They can also change our address to a new zip code.

You will see significant changes when you use your time wisely. It's also important to set aside time for development and creativity. There is also a benefit when we set aside time for family and self-care for a healthy balance. Time is exactly equal to all of us, no matter our status. There's no difference; we're given the same 24 hours, the same 60 minutes in an hour, and the same 60 seconds in a minute. But what you do with your time and what I do with my time can be drastically different. Time changes for no one. The clock is going to count whether we want it to or not.

The sun is going to rise and continue to set whether we want it to or not. This is considered a life cycle. These are just a couple of things that will not change no matter what in our lifetime.

When we don't do anything with our time, we'll find that a day or a week has gone by. Then, before you know it, years have passed. The sad part is that you may find that you are still sitting in the same place, with the same ideas and the same goals of which you haven't done anything to obtain them. When you're ready and when you're willing to make the shift, start with doing something amazing with your time!!! Write the vision and lay out the steps that will help you obtain your goals. Decide what needs to happen. You will quickly find out that it's not as hard as you thought it was. You'll find that achieving the plan is easier than you thought. When you want more, you will do more to achieve it.

The road to get there is right in front of you. So, let's do it, let's get up and make it happen. And if not you, then who? If not now, then when? Always remember, NO ONE else can beat YOU at being YOU.

Chapter 3

So, It Begins

One day, I decided to sit down and take a look at my finances. I wanted to make sure I was accounting for all of the money that I had coming in. The process included my job and businesses. You see, I wanted to evaluate where my money was going. You guessed it right, I created a budget. This was a sobering reality. This was the day that things got real. This was also the day that I had to face my truth... head-on. This day changed my life and awakened my mindset. Looking at all of the things I wanted to get accomplished and the amount of money I had left. It helped me to realize that something had to change. And initially, I thought that if I spent less money, I'd have more money. I even thought that if I cut back on some things that my bank account would grow. This included that if I cut out my clothes shopping that I would begin to see massive amounts of money in my account. Little did I know that it helped, but it was not enough. I still had more work to do.

One week it was ok to cut out spending and see some progress to my goal. But the next week, that was old because I wanted to get to my goal while keeping up with my current lifestyle. Seemingly, that was counterproductive. Does this sound familiar? Can you identify with this process? How many times have you seen this cycle in your life?

You see, the goals that I had set for myself were not happening as quickly as I wanted. Initially, I couldn't see how I was going to get it all done because my goals and my dreams were so big. Most people were telling me that my goals and dreams were impossible. What I didn't know was that most of the people telling me stuff had not accomplished what I was trying to do. So, of course, it would seem impossible. I knew that it was going to take a substantial amount of money to reach my goals. As I was sitting there looking at all that I had written down, I realized not only did I need to make some changes in my habits, but my mind needed an overhaul. My thoughts were telling me that it would take a long time to get to where I was trying to go. Not only was there a mental battle, but I wanted to look the part on my journey. It really seemed as if that was a part of my identity. My focus was out of sorts. When you write down your goals, you need to make sure that they make sense. Also, make sure that you view them regularly, it will be a constant reminder that it will take more than just saving money to reach your goals, but a mindset shift is the skill that is needed overall.

.At first, I thought I just needed more money. But what was I really doing? The plan that I came up with, the changes that I made, the cuts that I did, gave me several hundreds of dollars here and there. But what I really needed was thousands. Needless to say, I went back and did some more homework. I looked for new ways to make money. Once I made more money, that money could now work for me.

And this might seem a little strange or different. I started hearing things like scared money, don't make money. A dream is just a wish on the shelf if you don't do anything with it. A goal is just something that you want to do if you never take action to meet that goal. The way that I started viewing my association with money began to change over time. And that's how I came to know that the dollars that I was saving needed to have a purpose. It didn't need to go and sit in a bank account, accumulate and earn more money for the financial institution. This was a new way of thinking for me. I was always told to save all my money so that by the time I turned 65, I would have enough money for retirement.

Unfortunately, earning 10% on $1 doesn't accumulate very fast. However, when you begin to put your money in a position where it multiplies, you'll find that your money will makes astronomical gains. Some people call it quantum leaps. And that's a physical term. We'll find that when we put our money in a position to multiply, we will make millionaires instead of thousands. Because I started to associate with money differently, my thoughts transformed into how can I put more money in place to multiply for me so that I can get to my goals quicker? This allows me to see how it wasn't a sacrifice to cut those other things off, save a few dollars, and actually live by a budget. I was not bothered by that anymore because it became a lifestyle. The result of every decision can yield big results when applied with discipline.

Does it take thousands of dollars in order to achieve your goals? No. Well, it depends. Some goals will stretch you to the max, both financially and mentally. That should not be the determining factor if you are going to proceed forward or not. That should be the thing that pushes you. When your dream is larger than life, every mindset change and shift helps.

There's a part of our brain that's our protector. They call it the fight or flight syndrome; it will take off in a heartbeat if something scares us. In addition, we will become defensive instantly if something is going to hurt us. On the opposite spectrum we can become creative when there's something that we want. I will call this our quantum creativity. We can come up with an idea that is a game changer in the marketplace. Our mindset has infinite ability to help us sort things out in order to get what we want. Many of us are not ashamed of asking for help. But then, there are those that won't receive help because they're afraid, fearful and they don't know what's on the other side.

So, with our massive leaps in our creativity, we're able to build a bridge that takes us from one side of our equation to the other side. This creativity is available to all of us. Depending on where you are in your process, it may take you making some major sacrifices. Pardon me but let me ask a few questions. What are you willing to sacrifice to grow? What are you going to do differently to achieve your dreams? Does it take someone pushing you out of the nest? I am sure that you have some idea of what you need to get to that place or don't you? Taking the time to determine what to do next can be challenging, but self-reflection is a remarkable way to lay out your plan of action.

Write out your plan of action. Start by answering the probing questions at the end of the chapter to get you started.

_____

_____

_____

_____

_____

_____

_____

_____

_____

_____

_____

_____

_____

_____

_____

_____

_____

_____

_____

_____

_____

_____

_____

_____

_____

_____

_____

_____

_____

_____

_____

_____

_____

_____

_____

Chapter 4

The Process

Most people operate with a mindset that assumes success comes one step at a time. The seemingly unspoken but popular notion is that we must continue that process of one step at a time based upon our present level of success to the next level of success. As the blueprint states, we must go from step 1 to step 10 without missing a beat. The process does not look the same for everyone. So, why do we always try to put success into a one-size-fits-all concept? Success for you may be to make an additional $3-5k per month, and my level of success is to make an additional $20-25k per month. Either way, the look of success is personal and should be measured by the weight or emphasis that we have set for ourselves.

I don't know about you, but when I have reached a goal, I am so excited. I try to remember every step of the process so that I can do it again the next time. However, I have learned that the same process may not work from one goal to the next. This is where I have to be prepared to shift and pivot in order to grow. All of us have a journey we must take. Let's not make it harder than it has to be.

Many people go about their day-to-day events, trying to make small improvements in their success and performance. That can become mundane and like another routine when progress is not made. Having a process in place will help them measure how quickly they will get to the goals that they are trying to reach. However, many people don't realize that things won't go the same way every single time. When small changes and small improvements are put into action, it is possible to see massive growth. It is literally impossible to see growth when little to no changes have been implemented.

Have you ever thought about certain areas of your life that you have outgrown, and you can clearly go back and measure your progress, but in other areas, nothing's happening? For example: Some of us are the best workers when we show up at our places of employment. We're constantly excelling from one position to the next. But on the flip side, when it comes to our own dreams and goals, the momentum slows down. Even taking baby steps may seem like moving mountains.

Are you comfortable in your present situation with making small improvements? There is no right or wrong answer to this question. You have to be true to yourself. Your progress and determination are the results of your actions. You can push straight through to the other side and receive astronomical growth in a short amount of time by making better choices.

Do you want more growth consistently? You must be more disciplined and focused. These are the focal points you will have to hold on to tight. Discipline plus focus is the main stay of lasting success. For some people, the idea of moving to a higher level really scares them. These are the times when you become so consistent that failure is not an option. Before you know it, you are at that next level. So, whatever the thought process is that pushes you to get things done, that's the one that you have to constantly focus on. And more importantly, you've got to figure out how to stay in the flow. That's when the real success mindset has changed. Flow is the ability to move along steadily and continuously from one place to another without breaking the process. Whew!!! That's saying a lot without saying much. You have to get into the mindset that where you are is not where you will be always. There are no limits to where your flow and purpose will take you. The more that we limit ourselves or constantly resist progress, the more we miss out on opportunities to grow and prosper.

Look at this example for a moment... There are not certain elevators for elevation. What I mean is that we get on elevators with the expectation that it is going to take us to the floor that you select. You still have to select the floor that you are going to... If you never select a floor, you will never get to your destination. Therefore, if you never make a selection to shift, your financial mindset will continue to be in the same place and have the same results.

Some of us may need financial therapy and coaching to achieve the life-changing results we desire. There is nothing wrong with seeking support from someone that may have obtained the level that you are trying to reach. Financial coaching focuses on the emotional and psychological roots of financial behaviors that create stress in most families, individuals, and especially in marriages. Money is probably one of the top three reasons for divorce. The separation boils down to mismanagement of money. It breaks down further to not having open dialogue and conversations around money. What does the family budget look like? What are the family expenses? Are you having conversations to discuss big purchases, how much to spend for eating out, or buying gifts for each other? Having such conversations might seem like it is unnecessary until you have a financial problem to arise and the blame game kicks in. Finances have been the least talked about subject for centuries. Those that see the importance of facing the facts are well on their way to changing the narrative of their minds and legacy.

There is no time limit to start addressing the thoughts, the habits, and the mindsets related to your financial life. It's possible to begin where you are and develop real mindset shifts. If you're not following through with actions to change financial stability, your mindset is most likely to be blamed.

Our follow-through has to be on point first and foremost. We are no stranger to knowing that people perish for lack of knowledge. I've seen where people have obtained the knowledge and still have not achieved success because of not following through, due to a lack of determination, or they simply quit. The source of the ineffective mindset doesn't matter. But recognizing and addressing harmful money beliefs is highly important to your financial success. One shift in your mindset can enhance or limit your reality. It might only be a few faulty habits that are holding you back from your financial security and the dreams that you desire.

"Realizing that your actions, feelings, and behaviors are the result of your own mental images. Beliefs gives us the level that psychology has always needed for personality change. Once you tap into the power within, there will be no stopping your progress."

Chapter 5
Renewing Your Mindset

Has your life been one revolving financial challenge after another? Financial coaching or therapy might be just what the doctor ordered! Over 75% of Americans state that not having enough money is their primary source of stress. This is where you have to erase all preconceived notions of how you thought about money previously in order for you to renew and change your mindset. Financial therapy is a growing field and focuses on the emotional and psychological roots of financial behaviors that create financial stress. And this is where you get down to the source of what's causing the problem where things are out of order.

When you look at your spending habits, you have to look at your bills and analyze what's incoming and outgoing regularly. We call those assets and liabilities in order to be able to determine what's working and what's not working. For example, someone that grew up in poor surroundings might hoard money and be overly frugal. This type of person could be experiencing stress or anxiety when they overspend. While some issues may be better left to the professionals, there are many financial issues that can be fixed by self-therapy. Let's compare this to a weight loss journey. Many people are able to lose weight without a psychologist, dietitian, or personal trainer. And this is where they have sheer willpower, determination, and a renewed mindset that helps them through the process. When we break down the parameters around our mindsets, we can see that many habits will show up in areas of our lives that we may not have realized.

By addressing the mindsets, thoughts, and habits related to your financial life, it's possible to discover real changes. If you're not following through on the actions that you know will increase your financial stability, it is likely to be blamed on relying on old habits and techniques. The mindset that inhibits your financial results can come from many sources, such as: parents, teachers, news, erroneous personal observations, childhood trauma, including but not limited to your own personal experiences throughout life.

The source of the ineffective mindset doesn't matter. But recognizing and addressing harmful money beliefs is very important to your financial progress. In every area of your life, your mindset can create and limit your reality. I often say that a person's preconceived notion is a part of their reality. But once we start to learn where those thoughts come from, we can now deal with the source of the problem and build new habits to change and redirect our thoughts into a new mindset.

It might be only a few faulty habits that are holding you back from the financial security that you desire. How exciting is that? Imagine if you could speed up the hands of time to the new reality of what you want your life to be like. What would that look like? What would have shifted in your money mindset? What kind of house would you live in? What kind of car would you drive? If you had everything in order and money was no object, what would you do differently?

"Building new habits is a process. When you stop in the midst of something new, how will you ever know if it's going to work or not when you quit before the process is complete."

For this exercise, I would like for you to write out 7 to 10 challenges you have with money that is holding you back from living the life that you want to achieve. Then write out your plan of action to work on a resolution to overcome those challenges.

_____

_____

_____

_____

_____

_____

_____

_____

_____

_____

_____

_____

_____

_____

_____

_____

_____

_____

_____

_____

_____

_____

_____

_____

_____

_____

Chapter Six

Limitations

How your mindset creates and limits your financial reality.

Your beliefs and everything that you think about are the seeds that create your reality. Therefore, if you're thinking about being broke, that is going to be what your reality manifests. Your mindset affects your thoughts, which in turn will affect your actions, ultimately creating your circumstances. Changing your mindset can be the most powerful way to alter your life. Modifying your thoughts can change your entire life cycle. What I mean by that is you can literally change generations by shifting your mindset and actions.

A lot of times, it's hard to get a person that is set in their ways and their habits to change unless there's a benefit to them for their situation. Therefore, we have to look past where we are right now to see the long-term benefits of the shift. There are so many long-term benefits of this renewed mindset. Changing the habits that go along with this will help you to have that level of success that you desire. There are several ways that beliefs alter your financial behavior.

1. **Beliefs influence your self-confidence.** The set of beliefs you have about yourself, and your capabilities determines your level of self-confidence, and in turn, your confidence affects your ability to learn and apply new financial habits. This is where applied faith will make a difference. Faith solidifies that you can do all things. There's nothing that is impossible for you to do if you simply believe and have self-confidence. Confidence impacts your ability to pursue financial goals. If you're not confident in your ability to get results, you won't persevere. Having perseverance will keep you on track throughout your journey when you are working to achieve your goals. Faith will allow you to see yourself victorious and accomplishing your goals before you even get started. Mindset shift is not something that you start and then stop. You must keep going even when your shift is outside the norm or when no one will support you.

2. **Beliefs that alter our financial behavior is how we process information.** Scientists have found that people use new information to support beliefs they already possess rather than form new habits and

beliefs. If you believe that you can't save money, you'll look for evidence or ways to support that belief. I have seen time and time again where people give up because it seems impossible to do. We live in such a fast-paced society that we want change to happen overnight. I have heard that it takes 21 days to develop a habit, and as a result, real change happens. So, we must position ourselves to allow change to happen.

3. **Actions feed your beliefs**. We must know that it's literally impossible to rise above your mindset. If you believe that you'll never be wealthy, then you're right. You're absolutely right. If you believe you can't stick to a budget, you're right again. Therefore, it's so important to change your mindset to viewpoints that support your growth rather than limit you. Imagine yourself wealthy. Imagine yourself successful. You must see yourself being in the place that you desire every single day without doubt or fear of failure.

4. **Beliefs affect results**. Some people have been taught that money changes people for the worse. Having beliefs like this will prevent you from taking steps to accumulate a significant amount of

wealth. This is due to various reasons, including but not limited to feeling as if you're not worthy.

There is a place of prosperity that we all have the ability to obtain. There is a place for you among the elite. The elite are known as the two percenters. And that is a very small margin of the top wealthiest people in our society that have obtained the level of success that's available to all of us. There are only a small amount people in the elite clubs of millionaires and billionaires. Why is it that some people feel like being wealthy is so unattainable that they won't go after it? Don't settle for being a millionaire and not go after billionaire status. Realistically, being a millionaire is more common than not. This is not a theory, but it is a fact based upon increased wages and people going after higher levels of education. Businesses and institutions are willing to pay more to get people with advanced knowledge. And with great work ethics and the ability to get the job done, you will. Beliefs are the core of financial challenges. Enhanced beliefs lead to enhanced thoughts, actions, and results. Attacking your negative behaviors is the most effective route to success. Focus on your mindset, and you're more likely to enjoy positive benefits from your efforts.

Here are a few examples:

- I already have enough money.
- I don't need a budget.
- Making extra money will cut into my time.
- I'll have to work extra hard to make a lot of money.

It is a known fact that money equals freedom and time to do the things that you enjoy. The possibilities are endless as to what money will do for you and your legacy. There are many ways to change the course of your financial life. Your brain is a computer, and what you feed it becomes your reality. The fact that our brains can't tell the difference between the truth and a lie. It is our mindsets that helps us to distinguish the difference.

What are your beliefs about money? At the end of the chapter, I would like for you to make a comprehensive list of your beliefs regarding money. Be sure to include both positive and negative beliefs you will need this list later.

"The unreal is more powerful than the real because nothing is as perfect as what you can imagine. It's because intangible ideas, concepts, beliefs, and fantasies last. Stone crumbles, wood rots, flowers die, and people turn their backs on you. But things as fragile as the thought of a dream can go on and on."

Write out your comprehensive money beliefs:

_____

_____

_____

_____

_____

_____

_____

_____

_____

_____

_____

_____

_____

_____

_____

_____

_____

_____

_____

_____

_____

_____

_____

_____

_____

_____

_____

_____

_____

_____

_____

_____

_____

_____

_____

_____

_____

_____

_____

_____

_____

_____

_____

_____

_____

_____

Chapter Seven
Financial Check-Up

What it takes to achieve a state of financial health.

Financial Health isn't just about how much money you make. There are multiple components to financial prosperity and stability. People are earning over a million dollars each year and still have financial challenges. The mindset that income is all that matters is a limiting belief. Let's take a quick inventory. Do you have all of these financial components under control?

1. **Budget.** Whether you're earning minimum wage or running the most successful hedge fund the world has ever seen. Having a budget is still equally as important. Knowing how much you're spending and where the money is being spent is important, there's no way around it. The information is invaluable to you and provides boundaries that ensure your financial success.

2. **An income that surpasses your bills.** If your bills outpace your income, you're going to have financial woes. The most likely long-term outcome is bankruptcy or finding ways to increase your income quickly. Everyone would be wise to increase their income and lower their bills and people that are serious about their budget know exactly how much money they have coming in and the expenses they are paying out.

3. **Build an emergency fund.** Life is neither perfect nor predictable. Sooner or later, an unexpected expense will occur. Many families are only a few weeks away from being homeless if sudden unemployment or a major expense occurs. And because the markets are so unpredictable these days, it is wise that you build yourself a healthy emergency fund. And I would say that it would be a good idea to set aside three to six months of expenses. Your emergency fund should include all expenses. It used to be okay to say that having $1,000 in your emergency fund was acceptable. However, a new set of tires can wipe that out. So, I'll say, let's think bigger and look at our expenses wisely.

4. **Minimal amount of debt monthly outside of normal household expenses.** No matter how much money you make, or you have in your possession, it

is very easy to create more debt than you can handle. And this is why it is really important to know how much money you have coming in versus your expenses. Avoid debt whenever possible, especially debt to purchase items that are consumable or lose value.

5. **Control your spending**. It's easy to spend more than you make. Are you an impulsive shopper? Do you like to purchase items that are out of your income bracket? Then, this is where you have to really reevaluate what's the cause behind that and what makes you feel like you need to live above your means. Determine whether you're an emotional buyer or whether you just like to keep up with others, AKA the Joneses. You must evaluate your emotional behaviors and put them into proper perspective.

6. **Save regularly**. Are you saving a percentage of your every paycheck? With regular savings, you could retire in style. And this is where you have to allocate funds to savings just like you pay bills. This makes you wiser, and it ultimately will make you wealthier. And never think that you're not saving enough. When you're saving something, you're doing it. That says a lot because that allows you to

have the stability necessary to continue to say regularly. A lot of people overthink the power of saving $100 regularly and just don't save anything because they could not afford to save more. This mindset has to stop. Just like you have to exercise to get into shape. You have to build your financial muscles one week, month, or year at a time. Start somewhere and look for ways to increase your savings over time. Having discipline is key.

7. **Investing in your future appropriately**. Savings is great but leaving your money in a savings account is less than ideal. Do your investing activities address your needs? Are you saving for retirement? Most employers today have 401K's, IRA plans, and different forms of retirement accounts. It's always a good idea to take advantage of those accounts because the employer will match a certain percentage. This is lovely because you will have the opportunity to save or invest your money pretax, which ultimately is a win-win situation. Consult an expert about investing or saving for retirement. There are a lot of great options to help you meet or exceed your goals.

8. **Insurance secures your legacy.** Obtaining the proper amount of insurance to prevent a financial

catastrophe is mandatory. Insurance could be invaluable in the event of a serious illness, fire, or death. Any one of those situations could derail the best laid out plans. You want to make sure that you budget this into your financial plans. This is one of the things that I have found that people hesitate to do. For whatever reason, our society does not look at insurance as necessary unless it is for the car. This is something that we need to change our mindset about and make it a priority. We need insurance in every family. There are no ifs, ands, or maybe someday about it. Families are often devastated by the death of a loved one because of the lack of insurance, period. This is often due to that person being the main source of income for the family. Having adequate insurance allows you to be able to afford the lifestyle that you currently have or better with the funds you obtain from the insurance policy in the event of loss of income. And if you think that insurance is expensive, you will quickly learn that it is well worth the investment over time. The earlier that you start your policy, you will find insurance is actually affordable. (Please note: Consult a licensed insurance agent for your specific situation.)

Now, look back at the list of beliefs and determine which of the above items are influenced by your mindset. You'll probably have several additional beliefs to add to your list now. But remember, earning a lot of money is a great advantage. But it's not sufficient on its own to ensure financial security. You should do more than just earn the money. Once you obtain wealth, what are you going to do with it? Are you going to spend it all? Are you going to save some for later? Are you going to invest some of it? What are you going to do? You get to decide exactly where every dime goes. Write out your plan of action to make sure that your financial affairs are in order.

What's the game plan?

_____

_____

_____

_____

_____

_____

_____

_____

_____

_____

_____

_____

_____

_____

_____

_____

_____

_____

Chapter Eight

Negative Money Mindset Beliefs

Eliminate everything that does not

serve you!!!

Let's consider evaluating your money beliefs. It's necessary to recognize which beliefs are negative and which are positive. Positive beliefs are those beliefs that allow you to positively affect the eight components necessary for financial health. Negative beliefs get in the way of addressing the things that are important. Review, the eight components of mindset beliefs that may keep you poor if you are not careful.

1. **Rich people are greedy**. Some rich people are indeed greedy; however, some poor people are greedy too. Many rich people became rich through kindness and helping others—whether or not you're greedy, that's up to you. The important thing to remember here is that you don't allow greed to become you. Don't get so consumed by obtaining money that you forget about serving people to the best of your ability.

2. **You don't deserve to be wealthy.** Everyone that creates value deserves to be wealthy. If you're currently in a minimum wage job that you dislike, you can change your financial circumstances by creating value and charging the world for it. The decision is up to you. You have to want to make a change in your situation to get better results.

3. **You don't know how to create wealth.** Consider doing things that others don't like to do, but you love to do it. For example: Lawncare has become 6 and 7 figure business empires because people don't like to cut grass. Fulfilling a need can be the fastest way to wealth. There are numerous ways to accumulate wealth. Accelerate your path to wealth by doing what is enjoyable for you. When you are doing things that you love, you will do it for free. Just do more of it by helping someone else to become more efficient and then you can charge them for your services. Remember, fair exchange is not robbery.

4. **My friends won't like me if I'm wealthy.** It's common to find new friends as your life situation evolves. Some of your friends might not like the fact that you're wealthy, but your true friends will be happy for you, regardless. Every stage in your

life has the potential to influence everything about you, including your circle of influence. You should not allow yourself to become overly consumed by what people think. There is a little-known fact that everyone will not be happy for you, no matter what. There will be some who will relish the fact that things didn't work out for you. So, why not make the choice to become wealthy by being so good, they will follow suit by pursuing their dreams. Let's all get paid for doing the things we love.

5. **Money will change you**. Money has the ability to change everything about you. Who would not move if money was not a problem? Who would not update their transportation or wardrobe if they could afford it? Most people look forward to the day that they can change some things about their situations. Money provides opportunities and choices. It is your heart and mindset that still remain the same. The real changes happen on the inside of a person that makes the difference. Have you met some wealthy people with bad attitudes? Money can change a lot of things, but integrity and soundness of mind can't be bought.

6. **You can't be spiritual and have a lot of money.** Many religions espouse the belief that being poor is somehow looked upon more favorably by the powers that be. If you are looking to convert a population that was 99.9% below the poverty level, you'd probably say the same thing. People are not willing to follow those that are struggling themselves. It takes money to care for ministry and provide for those that are working full-time to care for the household of God. It takes money to do outreach and provide for the needs of the community. What happens when money will allow you to engage in more spiritual activities? If you've had an unlimited amount of time as the result of financial freedom, what would you do differently? How would you serve the kingdom? (Knowing that the kingdom is not in the four walls of the church only) Let's take a note from the book of millionaires and position ourselves to make a difference in the world through giving.

7. **You will be disrespecting your parents or elders if you make more money than they do.** Most parents would be thrilled to see their child(ren) do well. When we think about it, our parents want us to be successful. Parents want you to go after your dreams. Nobody wants to see their loved ones go

through some of the challenges or struggles they experienced. Use your access to the cheat code and learn from others and bypass some of the heartache or headache to success. Ask questions from those that blazed the trail before you to gain experience. It can be challenging not to get caught up in tradition. Learn from it and walk the path to success.

8. **It's hard to make a lot of money.** It can be hard to make any amount of money depending on the type of work. Most people that make moderate incomes complain about work. If you're going to work, why not get paid for being great at it? It's not too difficult to enhance your career. People position themselves to make more money by getting advanced education all of the time. Those that learn more often earn more because of the wisdom they gain for their efforts. The more you educate yourself in money and mindset, you will feel confident with the decisions you make to earn more. Making money is as much of a skill as saving and investing it. There are plenty of resources that can help you learn how to handle money wisely. Do your research carefully.

Do you have any of these common beliefs about money or yourself? If you hold beliefs that inhibit your ability to address the components of a healthy financial situation, your shifts in thinking will be more

challenging than necessary. You'll sabotage yourself

by neglecting the habits necessary to achieve financial happiness. This is where you must be truthful with yourself. The 8 mindset beliefs I provided is a small snapshot of what some people think about money that's negative. The list is exhaustive. What are your thoughts? What negative mindset beliefs do you have?

Take a moment to write out your money beliefs. Yes, you will need them later. The beliefs you have today have the power to create and the power to destroy. Human beings have the awesome ability to take any experience in their lives and pursue it with passion and purpose.

_____

_____

_____

_____

_____

_____

_____

_____

_____

_____

_____

_____

_____

_____

_____

_____

_____

_____

_____

_____

_____

_____

_____

Chapter Nine

Positive Money Mindset Beliefs

Positivity is not only contagious, but it is necessary for growth.

Positive mindsets are beliefs that will accelerate you along your path to financial independence. Creating such positive habits will be easier to have a greater financial future by shifting your thoughts. These mindset shifts can literally make you rich. Those habits can create generational wealth and a sound legacy.

1. **Money is the result from providing value to the world.** It doesn't matter how educated you are or what you look like. Everyone has an equal opportunity to be financially successful. If you provide value and charge people for it, you will receive a corresponding level of compensation.

A brain surgeon makes more than your average store clerk because a surgeon is providing more value. The CEO of a Fortune 500 corporation earns more than a brain surgeon for that same reason.

What are your values? What's your time worth to you? That's something that you have to decide along the way. I have heard it said, "Time is Money." I believe it.

2. **Money provides freedom and choices.** Money is great for solving problems and providing you with options. Maybe, money can't buy you love, but enough of it can fix a bad situation. Money can buy your ticket to Fiji or Hawaii to play golf all day instead of working. Money will give you the freedom to decide on what you want to do, when you want to do it, and how it will be done.

3. **Money will allow you to help others in a greater way.** It is a fulfilling feeling to know that all of your financial needs have been properly paid off. Then, you delight yourself in the ability to serve others with their financial challenges or assist them with obtaining their goals. And this is where giving really takes on new meaning, and it becomes a priority. True givers AKA philanthropists don't worry about what they will get in return. Philanthropists give because it's out of the goodness of their hearts and the calling they have to transform lives.

4. **Financial freedom will happen when your actions and mindset create responsible money habits**. Decisions like that are necessary to do anything spectacular. Simple actions taken regularly will result in great wealth. There is not always a magic formula to achieve great results. Your path to success will be based on the choices and decisions you make along the way. Embrace it and be intentional.

5. **Saving money can be easy and enjoyable**. How would your saving activities change if you believed saving was easy? What would you do differently? What would be your expected outcome? What would you do if money was no option in the next 3 to 5 years? Would you still save a portion of your money if you won the lottery or received a huge inheritance? Would you be frugal and live on a budget? Finally, what would you change about how you handle money? Truth is 70 percent of people who come into large sums of money without financial education or structure, will go broke in 5 - 10 years.

6. **Budgeting can be beneficial to your financial health**. If you struggle to create or stay with the budget, this mindset thought will help. Never think

about how challenging it could be. Think about the positive results that you want to get out of it. To create an effective budget, be sure to include all of your expenses and sources of income. Remember, you can't obtain your goals if you can't see where you are going.

7. **The practice that you only buy things you need.** How would your bank account look if you lived within your mindset belief? How much more money would you have? Would this practice be practical and effective? There are some goals that you will have to make some sacrifices in order to obtain it. How you process the choices you make can propel or hinder the timeframe of your results. You know what will work for you and your situation. Let that be your guide. Measure the results against your results and adjust accordingly. Do you have more positive beliefs than negative beliefs about money? Great!!! If not, you already know that there is work that needs to be done. Can you see how your thoughts about money are affecting your financial situation? Awesome! Now, it's time to take action.

8. If you want to enhance your finances, eliminate negative thoughts and replace them with a positive plan of attack. Do something about it!!!

Go ahead, write out what you need to change and why you want to change it. Be honest with yourself...

_____

_____

_____

_____

_____

_____

_____

_____

_____

_____

_____

_____

_____

_____

_____

_____

_____

_____

_____

_____

_____

_____

_____

_____

_____

_____

_____

_____

Chapter 10

Reprogram your Mindset

When you put good information in, you will get good information out!!!

There are many ways to address harmful beliefs and replace them with positive ones. Many times, all that is required is a little attention and an open mind. This is where you have to put away any preconceived notions and all of the conventional ways that you think things will change. The truth of the matter is that everything that you've been doing up to this point has gotten you to where you are right now. And in order for you to get past that point, you have to change some things, starting with the way that you process. Knowing this, if you continue to do the same actions, then guess what, you're going to continue to get the same results.

So, why not try something different. It's time to break open the "In case of an emergency box" and start on something brand new. This is how you will get to your next level. So many of our beliefs are created during childhood, and we've never questioned them. At one time, you believed in Santa Claus or the Easter

Bunny. It's likely that you have several beliefs about money that are impractical too. As a child, you didn't have the knowledge to determine how Santa came down the chimney or how the Easter Bunny was able to lay some colorful eggs around for us to find.

The older we get, the more we may question things. Why did I believe that in the first place? When we are taught new things initially, we don't question the origin until after we have applied the information. This brings me to the conclusion that most people view money the same way. It's easy to see how our environment influenced our decisions. We learned many skills from our parents, teachers, and friends based on the information that was handed down to them. The truth of the matter is that if it did not work well for them, why would it work for you? The cycles will continue the same way until you learn that there is a different way that serves you better. If you change just one thing in the process, your new journey will begin.

Many behavioral experts can't agree whether beliefs can be changed in an instant or whether it takes a significant amount of time. However, they like what the old Chinese proverb says, "The best time to plant a tree was 20 years ago; the second-best time is today. What happened in the process was that the tree grew over the last 20 years, and it matured. There comes a time when you can start a new tree and some new habits by the seeds that we plant." Today is a great day to make change happen.

Neuro Linguistic Programming

John Grinder and Richard Bandler developed neuro-linguistic programming, which is called NLP, in the 1970s. You may not be as familiar with their names but more familiar with great motivational speakers, who made the technology popular. Though there are many facets to NLP, we're most interested in the use of language and perception to change beliefs. For instance, if you imagine something that frightens you, the way you imagined it has an impact. There is an infinite number of ways to think about a spider, for example. If the image of a spider in our mind is very large and colorful, it will have a different impact on your emotions than an image that is small and lacks color.

The characteristics of mental images is called sub-modalities. These include the visual, auditory, and aesthetic details of a mental image. Now, follow this process to change your mindset with NLP.

1. **Identify a belief you would like to change.** Let's pretend you believe that you can't save enough money each month to ever make a difference. You change this belief by taking the action of saving. This means that you will cancel out the belief by overcoming the belief.

2. **Consider an old belief that you no longer consider being true.** Perhaps you once believed in Santa Claus or that you would have a hard time learning how to ride a bike. Notice the sub modalities of this once held mindset. This one could be tricky because the thoughts of Santa Claus and riding a bike may have come from your parents at an early age. The beliefs that are imposed on you, especially at an early age, can be hard to overcome. Many families teach and train young children to honor and respect tradition. Along with the traditions comes the emotions built up around the event. You will find that some people continue to have the beliefs they possess based upon how an event makes them feel happy or sad. The reason this could be challenging to overcome for some people is because of the emotion tied to the event. This could possibly be challenged by creating new beliefs with similar feelings of emotions. Start to think about how you

feel when you are faced with challenging your beliefs as you continue to shift your mindset.

3. **Think of something you know to be true**. It could be the belief that Christmas is on December 25th or that dropping a bowling ball on your foot will hurt. Take note of the sub-modalities for this belief or this mindset. The things that are known to be true are based on facts. Facts are the things that will not change surrounding the event.

4. **Think of a mindset that you like to add**. For example: It might be the belief that every penny saved is adding to your fortune. As small as a penny is to a million-dollar equation, it might seem so tiny that it could be overlooked. This time it's about the principle of these sub-modalities. Don't overlook even the smallest detail. Every step matters!

5. **Now think about the mental characteristics of a mindset that no longer serves you**. Think about how you'd like to eliminate it.

6. **Now alter the sub-modalities of the belief (in step #5) you'd like to eliminate by rewriting it**. Every penny saved is one step closer to my million dollars. Make your desired belief have the same mental

characteristics as the belief you know to be 100% true.

7. **And now, the test**. How do you feel about the original belief (in step #5) vs. the new belief (in step #6)? Can you feel a change? The ultimate test is to observe your behavior. If your behavior changes, you know you're on the right track. Many people find this process highly effective. It is possible to change a belief quickly with NLP. If NLP doesn't seem to work for you, there are always other options. ***Don't be afraid to seek professional help when needed. ***

"The only thing that permits human beings to collaborate with another person in a truly open-minded way is their willingness to have their beliefs modified by new facts. Only openness to evidence and argument will secure a common world for us. Your destiny could be attached to a new direction."

Let's go one step further with something else that you can practice. Change your mindset with logic. Humans are thinkers, and we can use logic to our advantage. Beliefs are interesting things. We can be influenced to believe anything. We're ultimately the creators of our beliefs. You can't see or touch a belief in the real world. No one can give you a belief you don't accept. Use the power of logic to shake the foundations of your harmful beliefs and mindset, thoughts, or challenges.

1. **Choose a belief you'd like to change.** For example, we'll look at a potential belief. "People that have lots of money are evil."

2. **Where did this belief come from?** Did it come from your parents, a minister, a teacher, or a neighbor? Did you read that money is the root of all evil? Knowing the origin can help you to change that particular mindset.

3. **Is this source an expert?** In reality, only a person that has a lot of money would have the experience to make such a statement. Your parents may have made such statements, and because they had authority over you would be the reason you believed it without question. And that is quite often a question that you may have to do a self-

assessment. Meaning some of the beliefs, habits, and even the mindset that you have now came from somewhere. You may have to go back and evaluate where you picked up some of those values. Where did you pick up some of your character traits, and thoughts that you think pertaining to money? For example, did your thoughts come from a person of influence that struggled with money? You can clearly see how you developed your thoughts when you see a pattern. You can go even further by doing a deeper evaluation by finding out where your person of influence may have picked up that mindset that was evidentially passed on to you. This would serve you by changing the narratives of those thoughts as you progress forward into your future.

4. **What is another possible explanation?** Money may be the root of all evil, but what other explanation could there be? Maybe, your current mindset is the explanation.

   - Maybe, you just heard that money is the root of all evil so many times that you believed it without questioning it.
   - Maybe, you observed that money gives evil people the chance to be evil. But does that mean that all people with money are evil?

5. **Realize that we form many mindsets, beliefs, and thoughts in childhood that fail to hold up to examination.** It's understandable why a child would form a certain belief under the conditions of childhood; those in similar situations would likely draw the same conclusions.

6. **Can you see that any of the other interpretations could also be the truth?** So, what is the truth? It's whatever fact you choose it to be. You are the creator, and your mindset is merely your creation. You interrupt ideas and experiences and assign value to these things. Find an interpretation that makes sense but also works for you rather than against you.

Faulty beliefs and mindset can be easy to change because they have the advantage of being incorrect. Most of our thoughts that stand in our way, can't stand up to scrutiny. Challenge yourself to evaluate the thoughts you have about a particular subject. For example: When you examine your beliefs around money, put your thoughts to the test and find out how they measure up. If you think that money makes the world go around, then evaluate that, or if you say that having an extra $100,000 a year will change things for you. What you think about matters.

"When it comes to controlling human beings, there is no better instrument than lies. The fact is that humans live by beliefs. And beliefs can be manipulated. The power to manipulate beliefs is the only thing that counts to them. Change every lie into the truth, and you will prosper."

Chapter 11

Cost-Benefit Analysis

Let's do a cost-benefit analysis on your mindset.

You probably made lists in the past by writing down the pros and cons of your available options. Why don't you do the same with your mindset? When you realize what a particular belief is costing you, you will have greater motivation to address it. It's the same way with your money. If you know, for example, that having bad credit can cost you thousands of dollars more than your counterpart with good credit, it will make you want to do something about it. And when you look at good credit and bad credit, there's not an apples-to-apples comparison there. Unless you are both in the same categories of excellent, good, or fair credit there's nothing to compare. Even then the odds of being exactly alike is rare because there are too many variables. That's the only way that you can do an apples-to-apples comparison.

It's also important to take note of what you gain or lose from your mindset because it could be holding you back or helping you to move forward.

Review the steps below to analyze the cost and benefit of your money mindset.

1. Choose a thought or a belief that you wish to change. Consider this mindset. "I'll never make $100,000 a year." What is this mindset costing you? Review the examples to see how they compare to your thoughts:

- If I don't believe I can make $100,000, it's unlikely I ever will.
- I'll be stuck in my current income bracket for the rest of my life.
- I don't have hope for the future.
- I'll never be able to buy the house I've always wanted.
- I'll never get to retire since I don't have any money saved.

2. Evaluate whether or not these beliefs are reasonable or unreasonable?

- Few things in life are 100% true all of the time.

- I can't predict the future, so how could I possibly know how much I'll make someday.

- Advanced skills and hard work in my current situation are irrelevant?
- My mindset will help me to become successful.

3. **It is a known fact that lots of people with fewer skills, less intelligence, and less education have made over $100,000 per year.** In fact, some of the wealthiest people in the world dropped out of college. That may be true for them but mind your business when it comes to what works for them as it may not work for you. Please take time to evaluate your situation accordingly.

    It may seem like there's nothing magical about $100,000. It's just a round number that looks good to our brains. Of course, $100,000 definitely looks good in your bank account, don't get it twisted. If you were given $100,000, I am pretty sure you would not give it back. I will confidently answer for you by saying, I know I don't have to ask you to find out.

4. **What do I gain by holding this mindset?** In most cases, you will find that those seemingly harmful mindsets have a disadvantage. That disadvantage is often adhering to fears and

continuing to be lazy. If you don't think you can make more money, you won't. Those harmful mindsets often prevent you from taking action.

A lot of people don't take action to change due to fear of not knowing what's on the other side of the process. Then there are others that simply don't want to put in the work. So, don't let that be you. Don't let your beliefs and your mindset hold you back from living a better life. Hold on to what you see for yourself in life. Be your own cheerleader when needed. This will help you to stay focused on your goals.

5. **What would I gain by adopting a more positive mindset?** How would you benefit if you believe that you could make $100,000 in the future? Check out a few of the possibilities of being positive...

- I would greatly increase the likelihood of reaching $100,000 extra income level with a plan.
- I have hope and enthusiasm to exceed my goals in the future.
- When I work harder, my job will be more secure from my increased effort and contribution.

- So, why not do that now if you know that $100,000 could literally change your life, especially if working a little bit harder is going to allow you to achieve extra income. Make the decision to go after it. Think about it. How can you increase your job security? How can you increase your goal of being debt-free? How can you increase your goal of having good credit except by putting in the work?

6. **Create an affirmation list**. Since your new mindset is positive, constantly remind yourself of the future regularly. For example: "I will earn $100,000 per year."

- Repeat your affirmations 20 times each morning and in the evening before you go to bed.
- Avoid discounting the effectiveness of affirmations. First, you must change your mindset. When you read about millionaires and billionaires, they use affirmations as a highly effective regimen. It's no secret that many of them use affirmations and manifestation at the top of their list of things that they do regularly. Now, try a simple experiment and apply affirmations to a simple task that you would

routinely avoid, perhaps getting up the first time your alarm goes off.

For example: when you hear the alarm, turn it off and repeat "I'm Getting up, full of energy and ready for the day." Say that over and over again. You'll find it much easier to put your feet on the floor! Remember, changing your mindset takes effort; merely understanding the processes won't accomplish anything. It's necessary to apply the new practices you put in place quickly. This is where you cannot cheat the system—this is where you begin to put in the work.

Write out your affirmations. That's right... let's start right now...

_____

_____

_____

_____

_____

_____

_____

_____

_____

_____

_____

_____

_____

_____

_____

_____

_____

_____

_____

_____

_____

_____

_____

_____

_____

_____

_____

_____

_____

_____

Chapter 12

Don't Stop... Shift into Overdrive!

Making Mental Shifts will help you drastically. Reducing Your Stress Will Ultimately Make You Happier and More Productive & Successful.

There are many well-educated people who have found a way to love and prosper their job. Yet, many others in the same field will find a way to complain about everything involving their work.

You see, the first group is at the peak of their career, overseeing large projects and climbing the corporate ladder by leaps and bounds. The second group is sitting back, observing the first group progressing. Some have even lost many jobs over the years as a result of such behavior. This brings me to the notion that mindset and attitude have a lot to do with the difference.

After all, attitude is powerful and infectious. People grow when they are in the proper environment. It is not by mistake that the first group is progressing by leaps and bounds. You owe it to yourself to be positioned in the right environment to feed your mindset. When you find that what you are doing now is not working, you need to realize it's time to change. Point blank and simple. When you see that everyone else is moving around you successfully, then start moving, and you will achieve higher levels of success as well.

It comes down to this... You cannot control what happens around you all the time, but you are in full control of how you choose to experience it. For example, you can choose to see the worst or the best in people and in every situation. You can choose to feel overwhelmed by what's on your plate or to feel energized and excited about your life. You can dwell on what you dislike about everything or appreciate what you have.

When you find yourself in a negative thought loop at work, consider how a mental shift could transform your experience—and the experiences of those around you.

Here are a few mental shifts to embrace:

1. Shift the thought "What are people asking me to do today?" to "What is the most important thing I need to do today in order to have a productive day?"

When something pops up like an email or a calendar invitation to discuss a topic of importance, reacting quickly should come naturally. You want to be courteous and prompt, and, quite honestly, it will help you to be more productive. Don't allow things to sit and linger for long periods of time.

But, of course, the email could keep you busy all day. So, plan out your day accordingly. Force yourself to decide in the morning how your day will be spent productively. Urgent messages aside, create a 5 p.m. deadline on your calendar to achieve "zero inbox emails." This will remind you to clear out your emails by the end of the day if you don't respond immediately.

This process will also work for any other tasks for the day. Schedule time for all of the tasks that you would like to get done for the day. Set reminders to help you use your time wisely.

This approach could be challenging at first, but repetition will help you develop good habits with your mental shift. If you love being responsive, then this mental shift might not be as hard to put into action quickly.

Ask yourself the question, "Have I already accomplished the most important thing I need to do today?" Until the answer is "yes," focus maniacally on it.

2. **Make the mental shift from complaining about your situation to finding what you love about it.**

Do you know many successful people that constantly complain about everything? I don't. Whether you work 30 or 60 hours a week, we all spend a lot of our waking hours at work and interacting with people on a regular basis. Surely, there's something to appreciate about your job and coworkers. Gratitude has a way of putting imperfections into perspective, so you can focus on exuding positive energy.

This mental shift affects those around you. People with positive attitudes are far more likely to be admired, respected, and promoted.

3. **Shift the thought "That was my idea!" to "I am a great team player."**

Having a bad attitude can be toxic, draining, and distracting. For some people, a bad attitude can easily develop when one person feels like their idea was taken by someone who gets credit and praise.

When you believe someone got ahead at your expense, it can be hard to let it go. But the sooner you let it go, the sooner you can make this mental shift. Focus your success by providing great work, knowing that your time will come.

Stay focused and knock the assignment out of the park. Come up with great ideas. Execute flawlessly each time. Focus on future results — not on who got credit for your idea.

And remember that everybody loves a team player. Make it a point to excel at work, support others, and let your great results speak for themselves. It's a much happier way to be successful. People appreciate those who do good work and celebrate the success of others.

4. *Make the mental shift from* "I'll just do it myself" *to* "Is there someone else who can do it better with less effort & more efficiently?"

It's smart time management to lean into your strengths and let others take advantage of theirs. It's also smart to delegate to those that can get the job done faster. This does not make you appear weak or unskilled. Let's imagine that you can now get twice the amount of work done in half the time with help. You are effective when you are doing the work yourself, but you are more productive with help.

When you're a leader, practice handing off tasks whenever possible. Not only does this free you up to flow in your creative space, but it also helps others to learn and grow. Imagine if you have more versions of yourself getting things done just the way you like it. That could be invaluable. Open yourself up to allow your creativity to flourish in your space.

5. Shift from "I don't have enough time" to "I have enough time to do everything I need to do today."

When work, household chores, or other

responsibilities pile up, it's easy to feel overwhelmed. But if you focus on what needs to get done, you'll find yourself effortlessly prioritizing those things, and accomplishing them will be what matters the most. Whenever you say, "I'm too busy" or "I can't get everything done," you're letting time manage you instead of the other way around.

Remember: Using mental shifts can change the tone of your day from stressed to empowered. You can take control of your time the same way. Practicing this can ease stress and increase your productivity with your time and allow you to experience more happiness.

Chapter 13

The Conclusion

It's Go Time

Now, let's put it all together with a simple plan of action.

1. **Determine the part of your financial life that's causing you the most grief**. Do you have a retirement plan, emergency savings plan, or budget? Are you on track to meet your financial goals? If no, ask yourself; Why not? What do you need to deal with to remove the hindrances?

2. **Make a list of all of the beliefs that are having the greatest negative impact on your financial life.** Which belief is holding you back the most or hurting you the most?

Here are some self-sabotaging beliefs:

-   I'll have plenty of time later.
-   I'm too young to worry about it.
-   I have to buy a house first.

- I won't live long enough to enjoy the fruits of my labor.
- It doesn't matter if I don't have a budget, retirement savings, or savings at all.
- I can't afford to save money now for something I won't need until later or, in the case of a retirement, for years.
- It's too complicated for me.
- I'll inherit all the money I could ever need.
- The amount I'm able to save won't make a difference anyway.

3. **Address them one at a time**. Pick the belief or the mindset that you think is creating the biggest obstacle and apply one of the techniques that we talked about earlier to eliminate that mindset and create a new one, which could be a more supportive belief system for you.

4. **Keep going until your behavior matches your desires, your wishes, and your goals.** It's impossible to feel better without taking action. Keep going until you're making the actual shifts in your mindset. You might have to try multiple techniques to have a greater have an impact. The techniques are not one-size-fits-all.

5. **Continue addressing all of your beliefs that don't support your financial future.** This will take time, but it's time well spent. When you are creating a mindset shift, you must constantly work at reminding yourself why you're changing & putting the work. Some of your "whys" may be that it is for you to have a better financial future or to create a greater legacy or retirement. Remember that your "Why" is bigger, and it's stronger than anything that you can put before it. What do I mean by that? Your "Why" is the thing that gets you up in the morning. Your why is that thing that makes you continue throughout the day. It gives you energy, and it makes your heartbeat fast, it will keep you passionate and excited.

There must be a shift in your mindset. Your mindset should be on your goals at all times when it comes to creating new beliefs and sustainable actions. A few simple steps taken each day will have a very positive impact on your future. Start by simply taking the first step!

"We learned our belief systems as little children, and then, we moved through life creating experiences to match our beliefs. Look back at your childhood and notice how often you went through the same experience. Don't keep going through the same cycles take time learn from them and change along the way."

There's a lot of information condensed in this book, but it will not become your reality until you make the mindset changes and put what you have learned into action. In order for you to shift your mindset, it is a wise choice to create some new habits and some new belief systems.

Ask yourself this question. Does your beliefs about money support you, or are they acting like a boat anchor weighing you down? We often know what to do, but we struggle to follow through and take the appropriate actions. Faulty thinking will inhibit your ability to address your finances successfully over a period of time if nothing is done to change.

Overall, negative beliefs alter your perception, your behavior, and ultimately your financial future. It's important to determine those negative mindsets and evaluate them. What would you gain by eliminating those negative beliefs and enlisting more helpful beliefs? Ultimately, you must change your mindset and how you think about money altogether. Changing your money beliefs can be accomplished by a variety of methods. Finding the optimal method is a matter of trial and error. It's important to get started immediately. Financial challenges rarely happen overnight, and the cure will take time too.

"Be flexible to evaluate and eliminate all of the limiting beliefs that have held you back from progressing forward. Don't settle for anything less than your personal best. No one should have to tell you that you have work to do. Allow yourself room to grow, make errors and work on your goals until you achieve them. Allow yourself enough grace where your efforts will pay off in the end. Change your money mindset and ultimately, <u>You Will Change Your Life</u>."

Chapter 14

Don't wait.

Write out your Expanded Vision Plan!

Journal about your vision. Compare where you are now and where you want to be 1, 3, and 5 years from now:

1 year from now, my goal is to:

_____

_____

_____

_____

_____

_____

_____

_____

_____

_____

_____

_____

_____

_____

_____

_____

_____

_____

_____

_____

_____

_____

_____

_____

_____

_____

_____

_____

_____

_____

_____

_____

_____

_____

_____

_____

_____

_____

_____

_____

_____

3 years from now, my goal is to:

_____

_____

_____

_____

_____

_____

_____

_____

_____

_____

_____

_____

_____

_____

_____

_____

_____

_____

_____

_____

_____

_____

_____

_____

_____

_____

_____

_____

_____

_____

_____

5 years from now, my goal is to:

_____

_____

_____

_____

_____

_____

_____

_____

_____

_____

_____

_____

_____

_____

What are your next steps? Write out your plan of attack? Be very detailed...

_____

_____

_____

_____

_____

_____

_____

_____

_____

_____

_____

_____

_____

_____

_____

_____

_____

_____

_____

_____

_____

_____

_____

_____

_____

_____

_____

_____

_____

_____

_____

_____

_____

_____

_____

_____

_____

_____

_____

_____

_____

_____

_____

_____

_____

_____

About the Author:

Dr. Tabatha Russell is a wife, mother, and grandmother. She is a multi-faceted woman that understands the power of shifting your mindset in order to achieve the unimaginable.

Dr. Russell has mastered that process of going from employee to CEO. She is an accomplished serial entrepreneur of several successful businesses that serve people to their highest.

After years of building businesses without real guidance, she understands the stress of not knowing how to properly set yourself up for success. Dr. Russell most certainly understands that money can be a catalyst or a deterrent. It all depends on your beliefs, perspective, and habits.

Dr. Russell holds 2 Doctorate degrees, obtaining one in Christian Studies and the other in Theology. Dr. Russell is an Adjunct Professor at Glory-to-Glory College of Theology and Leadership in Columbia, SC, and she is a Certified Master Life Coach. Dr. Russell hosts a weekly Internet Radio, Podcast, and YouTube TV show called: Inside Inspired Women on the Women Inspirational Network and Empowerment Network Platforms. She uses all of her knowledge and life experience to coach women to create 6 figure businesses from scratch in her exclusive Academy: **Breakthrough Millionaire.** Dr. Russell has made it her mission to uplift, inspire, and empower savvy business-minded women that lack confidence and guidance to harness their inner power in order to level up their price points, create multiple streams of income, and **Expand** their **Visions** while obtaining the life of their dreams.

Dr. Russell's motto: The only limitations are the boundaries of your mind. Otherwise, everything to be accomplished is fair game once put your focus & determination to it. Knowing this, we must be consistent and intentional to obtain success.

If you are ready to shift your mindset, put in the work, and create the life of your dreams.

The time is now... Your legacy is waiting!

Follow: FB: IamDrTabatha   IG: IamDrTabatha

www.IamDrTabatha.com

Remember, the time is now!

Let us help you go beyond accountability by helping you with a blueprint to bring your ideas to life through your business.

Ready to go to the Next Level Creating the Life you Desire.

Schedule a <u>Free</u> Discovery Session.

Coaching may be just what the doctor ordered.

www.IAmDrTabatha.com

Made in the USA
Middletown, DE
04 May 2022

65244665R00070